OCEAN ANIMAL ADAPTATIONS

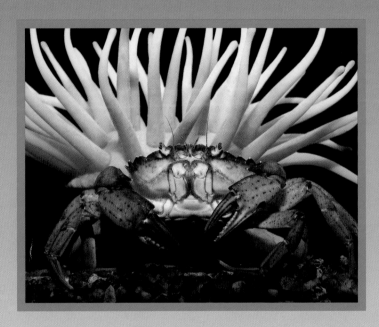

by Julie Murphy

Content Consultant
Jackie Gai, DVM
Zoo and Exotic Animal Consultation

CAPSTONE PRESS
a capstone imprint

A+ Books are published by Capstone Press,
151 Good Counsel Drive, P.O. Box 669, Mankato, Minnesota 56002.
www.capstonepub.com

 Books published by Capstone Press are manufactured with paper
containing at least 10 percent post-consumer waste.

Library of Congress Cataloging-in-Publication Data
Murphy, Julie, 1965-
  Ocean animal adaptations / By Julie Murphy.
      p. cm.—(A+ books amazing animal adaptations)
  Includes bibliographical references and index.
  Summary: "Simple text and photographs describe ocean animal adaptations"—Provided by
publisher.
  ISBN 978-1-4296-6029-7 (library binding)—ISBN 978-1-4296-7029-6 (pbk.)
  1. Marine animals—Adaptation—Juvenile literature. I. Title. II. Series.
  QL122.2.M86 2012
  591.77—dc22   2011004817

Credits

Jeni Wittrock, editor; Matt Bruning and Gene Bentdahl, designers; Wanda Winch, media
    researcher; Eric Manske, production specialist

Photo Credits

Corbis: Visuals Unlimited/David Fleetham, cover (crab); DigitalVision (Getty Images), 11,
12-13; fotolia: John Anderson, 17; Minden Pictures: David Shale, 21, Norbert Wu, 26; Nature
Picture Library: David Shale, 9; Photolibrary: Peter Arnold Images/Jeffrey L. Rotman, 25;
Shutterstock: Cigdem Sean Coop, 20, file404, cover, 1 (water design element), frantisekhojdysz,
5, Frederic Prochasson, 8, Mariusz S. Jurgielewicz, 14-15, Rich Carey, 18-19, ShopArtGallery,
28, tropicdreams, 22-23, Vladimir Chernyanskiy, 1, Vlasov Volodymyr, cover, 1 (coral design),
Zeamonkey Images, 4, zebra0209, 10; www.marinethemes.com: Andy Murch, 6-7, Mary Malloy, 16

Note to Parents, Teachers, and Librarians

The Amazing Animal Adaptations series uses full color photographs and a nonfiction format to
introduce the concept of animal adaptations. *Ocean Animal Adaptations* is designed to be read
aloud to a pre-reader or to be read independently by an early reader. Photographs help listeners
and early readers understand the text and concepts discussed. The book encourages further
learning by including the following sections: Table of Contents, Glossary, Read More, Internet Sites,
and Index. Early readers may need assistance using these features.

Printed in the United States of America in North Mankato, Minnesota.
032011   006110CGF11

TABLE OF CONTENTS

About Ocean Animals

Oceans are big, wet, and salty. They can be deep or shallow, cold or warm. Near the surface they have lots of light. But deep down, they are darker than night.

Ocean animals have special ways of
moving, hiding, and catching food.
We call these ways "adaptations."

Body Parts

The shark is a perfect ocean predator. Its bullet-shaped body slices through water. Its powerful tail makes the shark fast.

Chomp! Two or three rows of sharp teeth stop the shark's prey from escaping.

Penguins dive and dart under the water. They catch speedy fish and krill to eat. Their stumpy wings cannot fly, but they make fantastic flippers.

An anglerfish doesn't chase its
prey. It wiggles a pole-shaped
spine. Other fish think it's food.
When they come near—gulp!
The anglerfish snatches its meal.

Lying flat on the seafloor, this fish matches the sand. A flounder's two eyes are on its top side to watch for danger.

Sea stars have one eye on each arm. But they still have trouble spotting predators. It's a good thing sea stars taste terrible!

Anemones move very slowly.
But they can catch quick fish
with their stinging tentacles.

Zap! A fish is stung, pulled to the anemone's mouth, and eaten.

The stringy tentacles of sea nettles also sting prey. How do nettles blob, blob, blob through the water?

14

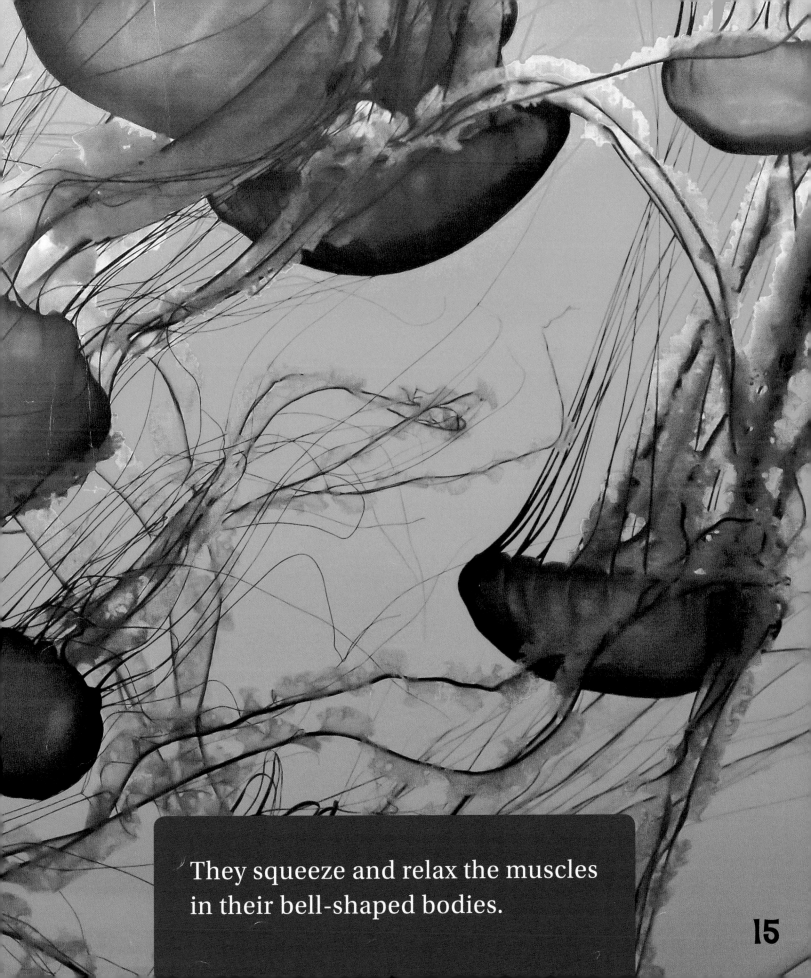

They squeeze and relax the muscles in their bell-shaped bodies.

15

Body Coverings

A gentle, leafy sea dragon hides from predators by sitting in seaweed. Leafy bits on its body sway just like its weedy home.

A decorator crab uses a disguise to hide. It sticks sponges, seaweed, and even small snails to its body.

Imagine changing your looks
to suit every place you go.
An octopus always blends in
with its ocean surroundings.

18

Dark or light, bumpy or smooth, an octopus has a disguise to match. Predators can't catch what they can't see!

This brightly colored sea slug doesn't mind being seen. Predators know the bright colors warn of bad taste.

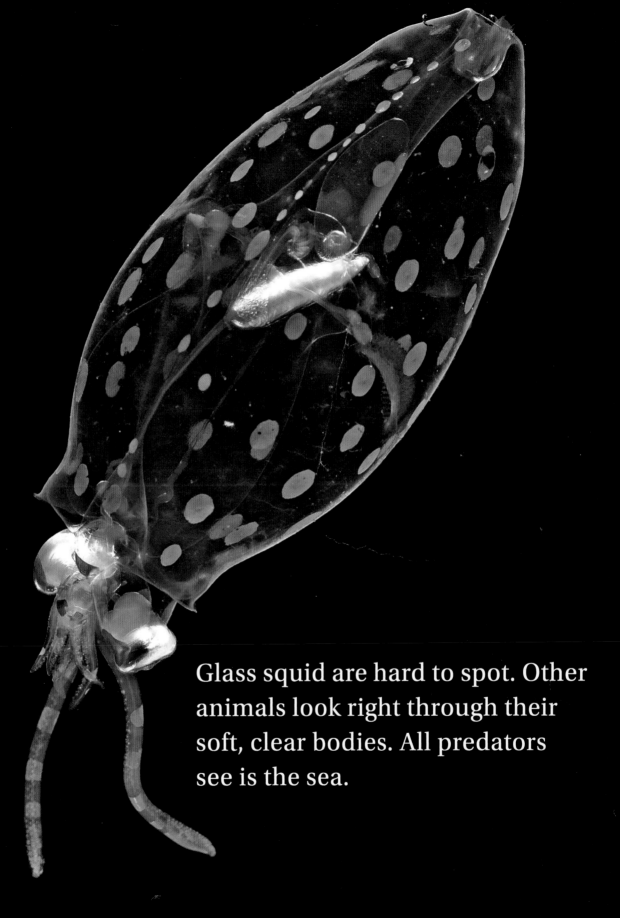

Glass squid are hard to spot. Other animals look right through their soft, clear bodies. All predators see is the sea.

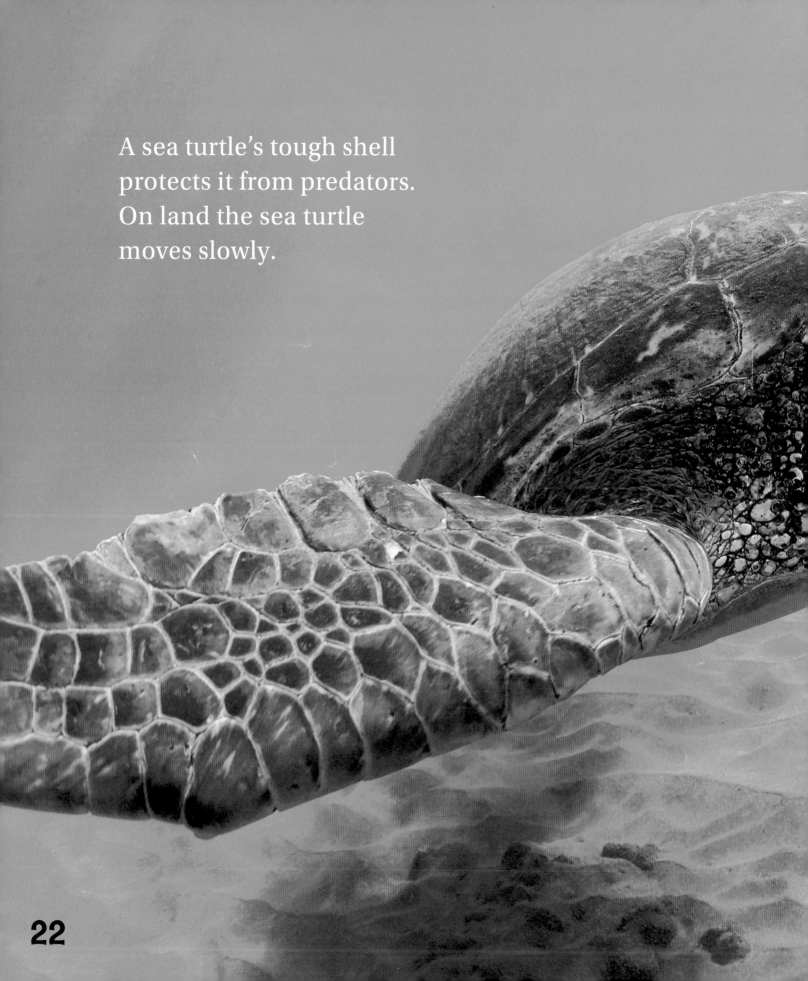

A sea turtle's tough shell protects it from predators. On land the sea turtle moves slowly.

In the ocean its shell feels lighter.
Turtles are strong swimmers.

Behavior

Sounds travel far underwater.
That's why hungry dolphins don't
look for food. They listen for it.

Hunting dolphins make clicking noises. The clicks hit nearby fish and bounce back. From the echo, the dolphins know where to hunt. Dinnertime!

25

A father sea horse holds his mate's eggs inside a special pouch. In his pouch, the eggs are safe. The tiny baby sea horses hatch and swim away. Good-bye, Dad!

This chart shows ocean adaptations mentioned in this book. Can you remember each animal's adaptation?

Animal	Behavior	Body Covering	Body Part
anemone			●
anglerfish			●
decorator crab		●	
dolphin	●		
flounder			●

Animal	Behavior	Body Covering	Body Part
glass squid		●	
octopus		●	
penguin			●
sea dragon		●	
sea horse	●		
sea nettle			●
sea slug		●	
sea star			●
sea turtle		●	
shark			●

Glossary

adaptation—a change a living thing goes through to better fit in with its environment

disguise—something that makes an animal look like something else

flipper— one of the broad, flat limbs of a sea creature

krill—a small, shrimplike animal

mate—the male or female partner of a pair of animals

pouch—a flap of skin that looks like a pocket in which some animals carry their young

predator—an animal that hunts other animals for food

prey—an animal hunted by another animal for food

spine—a sharp, pointed growth

sway—to move from side to side

tentacle—an armlike body part

Read More

Bessesen, Brooke. *Look Who Lives in the Ocean!: Splashing and Dashing, Nibbling and Quibbling, Blending and Fending.* Phoenix: Arizona Highways, 2009.

Dawson, Emily C. *Ocean Animals.* Our Animal World. Mankato, Minn.: Amicus, 2011.

Internet Sites

FactHound offers a safe, fun way to find Internet sites related to this book. All of the sites on FactHound have been researched by our staff.

Here's all you do:

Visit *www.facthound.com*

Type in this code: 9781429660297

 Check out projects, games and lots more at
www.capstonekids.com

Index